Doris Day: A Biography of the Famous American Actress and Singer

By

Sophie Miller

TABLE OF CONTENTS

Introduction 1

Early Life (and Disaster)......................................**3**
The Family 3
Dance and Disaster 4
The Discovery...5

Her Professional Start: 1938-1950 ....**7**
Doris Day Is Born...7
Big Firsts 8
Notes and Knots..9
The Big Screen...10

The Big Time: 1950-1960 ....**13**
Building Doris Day 13
A Free Agent 14

Career, Ruin, and a Nasty Surprise.......................**17**
Sliding to the Sidelines.......................................17
1968 19
From Big Screen to Daytime Television....................20

A Fizzling Career and a New Life: 1970-2000 ....**22**
Fourth Time's the Charm?...................................22
Doris Day: Her Own Story...................................23
Wrapping Up Loose Ends....................................24

The Legacy Years: 2000-2019...............................**27**
Award... 27
After Award...28
And a Public Appearance....................................29

Death: 2019 ....**30**

Marriages and Personal Life: Behind the Mask **31**
Her First Real Relationship – Or: Black and Blue 31
The Rebound...35
A Complicated Life 38
Third Time's the Charm 40

Fourth Time's the Charm? 41
Her Son's Brush with Insanity...42

Sexuality and Public Image....................................**44**

Animal Activism **47**
An Old Passion 47
A New Career 48
Political Activism 50
Activism into Old Age...51

Doris Day: Favorites **53**
Calamity Jane..53
The Man Who Knew Too Much and "Que Sera, Sera"...............54
"Day by Day" 55
"Sentimental Journey"..55

Introduction

Doris Day was beloved to the world as the quintessential 1950s woman. She was the blonde-haired, blue-eyed, "All-American Girl" that women aspired to be, and husbands wished their wives were. She was a woman revered by her fans, her critics, and aspiring starlets and stage actresses alike. Even after her death, the media celebrates Day's life and legacy as the gorgeous animal rights and welfare activist with the ultimate Hollywood start and classic "girl next door" persona.

The New York Times critic Charles Champlin summarized America's fascination with Day in a review published in 1988: "She conveyed a unique blend of innocent sexiness .... That was not so much the woman next door as the woman you wished lived next door."

Day had a reputation onscreen and in the media as being simultaneously sexual and virginal. Her characters and persona both maintained careers while appearing as "domestic" women, with the approachability of the clerk behind the counter, yet presenting an elegance reminiscent of more proper times. While Day outwardly enjoyed being the ideal 1950s woman, it became clear even to her that she was merely the epitome of a nonexistent, uncomplicated, uncomplaining image of modern womanhood.

Her persona was built to bely a career full of hard work, hardship, and hard marriages. At times, her superstardom only served as the antithesis of her private life, which was wrought throughout the years by physical injury, personal indignation, and financial ruin. She represented, to the public, husbands, aspiring housewives everywhere, a vanishing vision of what it meant to be the perfect woman. Yet, her own life served as the perfect example of an image of a woman far removed from reality. Day was, until the day of her death, the sexual virgin of Hollywood, the ultimate paradox of mid-century filmography and husbands' fantasies alike.

While the world often recognizes and celebrates Doris Day for her accomplishments onscreen and in the studio, Day would prefer to be remembered for her animal welfare work. Once she left the Hollywood life in the mid-1970s, she never looked back. She embraced her new life's mission: to protect animals and the people who wanted to protect them in turn. Day actively lobbied Congress for legislation on animal welfare and population control issues, worked to adopt out animals taken in by organizations she was associated with, and even pioneered Spay Day USA in 1995.

Day had a passionate love of animals from a young age and believed she had a soulful connection with each and every one. Famously, when she visited a horse that she sponsored through the SPCA, every other horse in the facility was drawn to her immediately. The staff at the center said they'd never seen their abused horses so affectionate with anyone, human or otherwise.

It was Day who summed up her life and her attitude about her work quite succinctly: "I think everything in my life led me to my animal welfare work."

Early Life (and Disaster)

"The one radio voice that I listened to above others belonged to Ella Fitzgerald. There was a quality to her voice that fascinated me, and I'd sing along with her, trying to catch the subtle ways she shaded her voice, the casual yet clean way she sang those words." – Doris Day

The Family

The woman the world knew and loved as Doris Day was born Doris Mary Anne von Kappelhoff on April 3, 1922, in Cincinnati, Ohio (though she believed until her 95th birthday she was born in 1924). Her mother, Alma Sophia, named her daughter after Alma's favorite silent movie actress, Doris Kenyon.

Day's father was William Joseph von Kappelhoff. She had two brothers. The eldest, Richard, died before her birth. Paul was two years older. Both of her parents were first-generation German-Americans with parents who had immigrated from before their births.

Franz Joseph Wilhelm Kappelhoff was Day's paternal grandfather and a German immigrant who came to the United States in 1875. He settled his family in Cincinnati, Ohio, for the city's large German community, at that time chock full of German churches, clubs, and newspapers.

William Kappelhoff, Franz's son, was a choirmaster and music teacher, as well as the church organist for St. Mark's Catholic Church. He loved classical music, opera, and pretty women. Due to his infidelity with his wife's best friend (among other women), he and Alma divorced in 1934, when Day was twelve. Joseph married and moved in with his wife's best friend shortly thereafter.

Alma Kappelhoff – maiden name Welz – was an outgoing homemaker who, in contrast to the sophisticated tastes of her husband, preferred "hillbilly music," as well as modern pop, country, and Western. After the divorce was finalized, Alma moved her children to Evanston, Ohio – a Cincinnati suburb – where they lived above the Welz bakery and tavern. Alma worked as a baker for the family business to support her children.

Though Alma was busy providing for two children, she always made time to encourage her daughter's abilities and pursuits, and she maintained a dominant hand in directing Day's career for many years.

Dance and Disaster

Doris Day developed an interest in dance sometime around age 6 and displayed a knack for both tap dancing and ballet. From a young age, Day intended to pursue dancing as a career. Her mother enrolled her in lessons at the Hessler Dancing School, where Day honed her craft and eventually formed a dancing duo with Jerry Doherty in the mid-1930s. A local Cincinnati dance contest win netted them a prize of $500 and a chance to travel to Hollywood. There, the young dancing stars networked with professional body movement artists and worked with the prestigious Fanchon and Marco stage show. When she wasn't performing, Day studied under the direct tutelage of Mr. Louis DaPron.

Alma was just preparing to move her family full-time to Hollywood so Day could seriously pursue her dance career when tragedy struck. The date was October 13, 1937. Day was 13 years old at the time, riding home in a car when the vehicle was struck by

4

a train at the High Street crossing at Fifth Street by a Pennsylvania Railroad locomotive. At that time, that crossing specifically, and most crossings in general, didn't have a system of warning lights or cross gates.

Day was one of four people injured. Her legs were crushed in the accident, and she ended up in the hospital with a shattered right leg and double compound fracture. If that hadn't been enough to end her career, the fall she took during her 14 months of recuperation definitely was. Day sustained a second round of damage to her right leg, which set her recovery back several months. The incident put her in a leg brace and a wheelchair and ended any visions she had maintained of pursuing a professional career in dance.

The Discovery

Day's family lived above her uncle's tavern, and her time off was spent mainly downstairs playing the day's hits on her uncle's jukebox, sitting in her wheelchair and rocking the time away. By the time she was fourteen, Day had acquired a fondness for swing music, especially stars such as the Dorsey Brothers and Benny Goodman, among others. Ella Fitzgerald was also a favorite, and soon Day found herself singing along with the jukebox and the radio, attempting to emulate and then adapt Ella's unique style.

Said Day of the time: "During this long, boring period, I used to while away a lot of time listening to the radio, sometimes singing along with the likes of Benny Goodman, Duke Ellington, Tommy Dorsey, and Glenn Miller. But the one radio voice I listened to above others belonged to Ella Fitzgerald. There was a quality to her voice that fascinated me, and I'd sing along with her, trying to catch the subtle ways she shaded her voice, the casual yet clean way she sang the words."

Alma's interest in showbiz rekindled with her daughter's singing, and so she offered Day the chance to take singing lessons with a local voice coach, Grace Raine. Three months into lessons, Raine told Alma that she believed Day to have "tremendous potential" and gave Day three lessons per week for the price of one. Day stayed with Raine for eight months, learning, shading, and perfecting her voice. Years later, she would come to say that Raine had had the most prominent single effect on Day's singing style and career. Day credits Raine with teaching her the importance of a well-delivered lyric.

It was during those eight crucial months that Raine used her connections to get Day an unpaid singing showcase on a local radio show, *Carlin's Carnival*, at the WLW radio station. The first song Day ever performed for an audience – albeit through the airwaves – was "Day After Day" by Arthur Schwartz from 1932. That was the song that jumpstarted her career, and it earned her a regularly featured spot on the radio station. Her newfound local stardom also found her singing in a Cincinnati restaurant, Charlie Yee's Shanghai Inn, for a short time.

Her Professional Start:
1938-1950

"The happiest times in my life were the days when I was traveling with Les Brown and his band." – Doris Day

Doris Day Is Born

Though Alma Kappelhoff and Grace Raine were Day's earliest mentors and sources of encouragement, it is Barney Rapp who might deserve the most credit for Day's initial ascent to superstardom.

Barney Rapp was an American jazz musician and orchestra leader. He owned the local Cincinnati nightclub "The Sign of the Drum." He was, at the time Day was singing on the radio, in the market for a new female performer. He became enraptured with her singing prowess while listening to her on the radio and asked if she would like to hold an audition for his opening. Day said yes and scored the job at only fifteen years old, unable to read music, and beating out more than 100 female applicants in the process. Pay started at $25 per week, about $450/week in 2020 dollars.

It was during her time working for Rapp in 1939 that Day earned her famous surname. Rapp felt that "Kappelhoff" was much too long of a stage name for marquees and billboard advertisements, as well as too "Jewish" a name for their customer base. As he so admired her performance of "Day After Day," he felt it was only appropriate she be named after the song that started her career. Though Day accepted the name, she expressed dislike and dissatisfaction with his choice, likening it to a headlining act at the Cincinnati Gaiety Burlesque House.

In late 1939, Day was informed of a vocalist opening in Bob Crosby's – brother of Bing Crosby – band. She was encouraged by her mother, among others, to audition for his orchestra and "Bobcats" at the Blackhawk Club. At 17 years old, she got the job. During this time, she worked with many of the sidemen who would come to work on her own records at the height of her stardom – Billy Butterfield, Bob Haggart, Zeke Zarchy, and William Stegmeyer, among others.

Big Firsts

Day stayed with Crosby for three months before she was approached by Les Brown in early 1940. Les Brown and his "Band of Renown" noticed Day while she was working a Crosby gig at Strand Theater in New York City. He approached her with an offer to join, and she, elated at the prospect of moving up in her career, accepted.

It was with her first stint with Les Brown that Day really became famous, as it was the first time the public at large would get to hear her voice and know her name – first on the radio, and then on Brown's recordings. Her voice was capable from a young age of captivating crowds of all ages around the world. She had a firm command on her shading, her tone, and her projection. It was said that she sounded like she was singing to each individual person in the audience, not a crowd en masse. Her records and performances resonated personally for every and each ear listening. She was an instant favorite for almost everyone who had the chance to hear her.

Day's first marriage was another major life-changer that came out of her time working with Les Brown. March 1941 saw her walk down the aisle to meet Brown's trombonist Al Jorden at the altar. The marriage was tainted by incidents of physical abuse and allegations of stalking and crazed jealousy. Day and Jorden had one son, Terrence "Terry" Paul Jorden, a few short months into their marriage. Al Jorden was not happy to be having a child and beat Day in an attempt to force a miscarriage when she refused to have an abortion. Day and Jorden divorced in February1943, and Day took her son with her. Jorden, who was later suspected of being a violent schizophrenic, eventually killed himself.

After the finalization of Day's divorce, she returned home to Cincinnati to once again join the WLW radio station. Shortly thereafter, she rejoined Les Brown and his traveling band in Columbus, Ohio, where she remained until 1946.

During her second stint with Brown, in the year 1944, she recorded her first hit: "Sentimental Journey." It quickly rose to the top of the charts, partly due to its role as an anthem of World War II as a vocalization of the desire to end the war and bring the boys home. Her first hit was soon followed by 11 others, as her popularity as a sultry singing sensation skyrocketed. Her songs portrayed her to the people as personable and accessible. Though her career was star-studded from start to finish, it was "Sentimental Journey" she would come back to record again and again throughout.

Notes and Knots

Less Brown once said that Doris Day belonged in the grand artistic company of personalities such as Bing Crosby and Frank Sinatra. She toured the United States extensively with Brown, as well as to complete weekly radio work on Bob Hope's program. From 1945-1946, while working with Les Brown and his band as a vocalist, Day deservedly had six more top ten hits:

- ▸▸ "My Dreams Are Getting Better All the Time"
- ▸▸ "Tain't Me"
- ▸▸ "Till the End of Time"
- ▸▸ "You Won't Be Satisfied (Until You Break My Heart)"
- ▸▸ "The Whole World is Singing My Song"
- ▸▸ "I Got the Sun in the Mornin'"

Day's second hit with Brown, "My Dreams are Getting Better All the Time," netted her a solo contract with Columbia Records in 1947. This relationship would last for 25 years. The months after her first album found her working on the radio with big-name stars such as Bob Hope and Frank Sinatra. It was her time on the radio that was ultimately blamed for her second divorce.

Day tied the knot with saxophonist George Weidler, brother of actress Virginia Weidler, March 30, 1946. Their marriage only lasted a short while. George watched Day grow from a small-time name into a rising star personality and decided he didn't want to become known as "Mr. Doris Day" for the rest of his life. He sent notification of the divorce to the Little Club in New York City, where Day was currently performing. Devastated, Day returned home to Los Angeles, but Weidler and Day were unable to work past their differences and eventually finalized their divorce in 1949. Though they would meet at a reunion some years later – where Weidler introduced Day to Christian Science – they didn't keep much contact throughout Day's life. Weidler went on to play with the Stan Kenton Orchestra, and then formed his own band in the early 1950s.

The Big Screen

It was in the midst of her relationship troubles with George Weidler that Day made her big transition from stage and radio to the big screen, in 1948. Though she was still despondent over the impending divorce proceedings, Day – having parted ways with Les Brown not long before – accepted, albeit reluctantly, an offer to sing at a star-studded Hollywood party. Among those in attendance were famous songwriters Julie Styne and Sammy Cahn. When Day was asked to sing, she performed a tearful, emotionally charged rendition of "Embraceable You." Her performance of the song so impressed the songwriting team of Styne and Cahn that they recommended her to try for the lead role in *Romance on the High Seas*. The film had been plagued by leading ladies – among these a pregnant Betty Hudson – dropping like flies for one reason or another.

Director Michael Curtiz asked Day to screen test alongside two actresses who had previously auditioned as a means of comparison. When Day walked onscreen for her audition, those present in the room immediately felt that she was The One they had been searching for – she was perfect! Curtiz offered Day the role, to Day's great shock. Day told Curtiz that she was a singer without acting experience and was therefore unqualified for such a leading role.

Instead of being talked into giving Day the boot, Curtiz told Day that he appreciated "that she was honest" and unafraid to admit her lack of experience. He told Day she fit his desired profile of a woman who "looked like the All-American Girl," and insisted she take the lead role of Georgia Garrett in the film.

Curtiz later came out to say that Day was his proudest discovery. At the end of filming, he placed her under a personal contract to continue filming with Warner Brothers. Once, he caught her taking acting lessons while filming her first movie – and he insisted that she stop, as everyone on set felt she didn't need them. Rock Hudson said of shooting with her on the set of her first movie: "Doris was an Actors Studio all by herself. Her sense of timing, her instincts – I just kept my eyes open and copied her."

Romance on the High Seas also provided Day with the opportunity to record her first No. 2 hit: "It's Magic," written by Sammy Cohn and Julie Styne. Her first soundtrack hit topped over a million sales and maintained a place on the Hit Parade for many weeks. Another famous hit of the time, "Put 'em in a box, tie it with a ribbon, and throw it in the deep blue sea" – also written by Cohn and Styne – is considered to be a significant contribution to the recording industry at the time.

A short two months later, Day recorded her first No. 1 hit, a duet she recorded with Buddy Clark in 1949.

During the early stages of her movie career is when she resumed her recording career as well in1947. The 1940s saw the jazziest qualities of Day's voice fall to the side. Still, her voice never lost its jazzy undertones, even as she expanded further into the world of slow ballads. Her musical work continued with the soundtrack *of Romance on the High Seas* in 1948, and again with *My Dream is Yours* in 1949, which saw Day record one of her most famous songs: "Someone Like You."

Day's musical and feature film professions continued to run in tandem and branch off each other for most of her superstar career. It was typical for the songs she sang in her movies to become famous hits in their own rights.

At the same time as Day was making her Hollywood film start, she was also engaged with Columbia Records working on hundreds of singles and albums. Between 1949 and 1955, Day had eight albums chart in the United States, only one of which didn't make it into the top five.

The Big Time: 1950-1960

"If you play the numbers game and become obsessed with it, as so many in Hollywood are, sooner or later, you have to face the depressing fact that if you are number one, the only place you can go is down." – Doris Day

During the 1950s, Doris Day was amongst the most popular and highest-paid singers in America. The burst of movie fame that followed her first two films and resulting adulation only furthered her impact on modern life and pop culture. And, although movies would soon come to eclipse her musical career, she remained deeply passionate about singing. Even in the midst of her merging professions, she still managed to return to her jazzy roots and record an album with Andre Previn, *Duet*. Day made a point throughout her film career to make time for solo musical projects. She even hosted her own radio program, *The Doris Day Show*, from 1952-1953 on CBS.

Building Doris Day

From 1949 to 1958, Day ranked as the No. 1 female on Billboard's annual nationwide poll nine years out of ten. As 1960 approached, it now seemed apparent that her popularity and success as a vocalist were quickly being eclipsed by her box office appeal. Day's screen persona was presented as that of an intelligent, wholesome, conservatively polite woman, maintaining traditional homemaker values while pushing a few boundaries in her career decisions. Her infallible optimism and understated strength of character saw her become the epitome of the ideal 1950s American woman.

While she later became known as the queen of the "sex comedy" – what we call romantic comedies today – Day spent much of the '50s proving her talents for more dramatic roles. 1950 saw her play a singer involved with a troubled musician, played by Kirk Douglas, in *Young Man with a Horn*, as well as a housewife married to an abusive KKK member in *Storm Warning* opposite Ronald Reagan (whom she very briefly dated). Her most successful film for Warner Brothers was shot in 1951 as her fourth round of tutelage under director Curtiz: *I'll See You in My Dreams*. The movie served as a musical biography of famous lyricist Gus Kahn and broke standing 20-year box office records.

Day's films quickly and frequently became top earners at the box office and in the recording studio both. As her feature films alternated between more dramatic and musical roles, her songs branched from ballads into more modern pop music. Between 1950 and 1953, Day saw six of her movie musical albums top the charts amongst the Top 10 hits, three of which hit No. 1, including "Secret Love" from the musical western *Calamity Jane* in 1953. The song netted an Academy Award for Best Original Song for songwriters and composers Sammy Fain and Paul Francis Webster. Day's recording raked in seven figures in a matter of months and was her fourth No. 1 hit single to top the Billboard charts in the United States.

A Free Agent

1951 saw Day make a significant personal life change in her marriage to her third husband on April 3 – her 29th birthday. Doris Day and Martin "Marty" Melcher married in a ceremony at Burbank City Hall. Melcher adopted Day's son from her first marriage, Terry, and life seemed to be going well. Terry adored Melcher (at first), and Melcher worked closely with Day as her manager and agent to see her through some of her biggest hits and best feature films.

After her husband ended her contract with Warner Brothers in 1954, Day found herself with a lot more freedom in her range of roles as a freelance actress. She played a fictionalized version of the 1920s singer Ruth Etting opposite James Cagney in the 1955 biopic *Love Me or Leave Me*. The soundtrack became a No. 1 bestseller in the United States, with "I'll Never Stop Loving You" by Sammy Cahn and Nicholas Brodszky topping the charts. The movie itself received critical acclaim and was a massive commercial success for both Doris Day and MGM. Day thought it was her best acting performance to date, and later said she believed it might have been her best film performance ever. Producer Joe Pasternak said that he was "stunned" Day didn't receive an Oscar nomination, let alone a win.

Perhaps the most famous song – and performance – of Day's career came out of Alfred Hitchcock's 1956 suspense/thriller *The Man Who Knew Too Much*, in which she starred opposite James "Jimmy" Stewart. "Que Sera, Sera (Whatever Will Be, Will Be)" saw an Academy Award for Best Original Song given to songwriters Jay Livingston and Ray Evans. Over one million copies were sold in a matter of months. The movie itself was Day's tenth film to hit Top 10 at the box office. Famously, during production, Day asked producer Alfred Hitchcock why he never gave her directions for method, style, or performance. Hitchcock's reply was simple: "You are doing everything just right." This once again proved to Day her natural abilities as a performer and an actress.

Actor James Cagney described her around this time as having "the ability to project the simple, direct statement of a simple, direct idea without cluttering it." He compared her performance to Laurette Taylor's performance in The Glass Menagerie on

Broadway – at that time, considered one of the greatest ever performances by an American actress.

Her next dramatic role was in the thriller/noir *Julie* in 1956, opposite Louis Jordan. While not as popular as some of her other films at the time, it still managed to draw in adoring crowds.

After her three successful, successive dramas, Day stepped back to the roots of her fame: music and comedy. Her next big film was a return to Warner Brothers with *The Pajama Game* in 1957, based on the namesake Broadway play, in which she starred opposite John Raitt.

Teacher's Pet followed in 1958, a Paramount Pictures comedy that paired her with Clark Gable and Gig Young. *Tunnel of Love*, another sex comedy, also came out in 1958. Both of these were successful movies in their own rights. *It Happened to Jane*, a 1959 role that set her opposite Jack Lemmon, found much less success.

Pillow Talk, another lighter comedic film in 1959 from Universal Studios, was her first onscreen pairing with Rock Hudson and Tony Randall and brought Day the only Academy Award nomination of her acting career, as well as a Golden Globe Award. The story focuses on Jan Morrow, an interior decorator who shares a multi-party landline with a playboy and Broadway composer.

After *Pillow Talk*, Day moved on to *The Thrill of It All*, playing a housewife who gains fame and notoriety as a TV pitchwoman to the great remorse and chagrin of her husband, played by James Garner.

Career, Ruin,
and a Nasty Surprise

"I just feel so fortunate and so blessed to have been able to entertain people in the theatres and on record, it's just an amazing life that I've experienced." – Doris Day

By the early 1960s, Doris Day had stamped her mark on the world as a cultural icon of the 1950s housewife. Between 1960 and 1964, she repeatedly ranked No. 1 female lead at the box office. The only other woman to achieve No. 1 four times in her life up until that point had been Shirley Temple. Day's record even now has yet to be equaled: she is the only top female box office star ever to receive seven consecutive Laurel Award nominations, and nine in total in 11 years – four of which she won. Between 1959 and 1970, Day received six Golden Globe nominations for best female performance in a variety of film roles, including comedies, dramas, musicals, and her television series.

Sliding to the Sidelines

1960 saw Day break her comedic run with Rex Harrison in the thriller *Midnight Lace*, a modern update of the stage thriller *Gaslight*. She starred alongside David Niven and Janis Paige in *Please Don't Eat the Daisies* in 1960 and opposite Cary Grant in *That Touch of Mink* in another return to comedy.

After Day's blonde, domestic wife career seemed to be coming to an end, she turned to star in a string of sophisticated non-sexual sex comedies.

The Thrill of It All and *Move Over, Darling*, both 1964 comedies, saw Day team up with James Garner twice. The theme song to *Move Over, Darling*, "Move Over, Darling," was co-written and produced by Day's son Terry, and the song hit No. 8 in the UK and gave her a Top 20 in 1964. The song's success was a wake-up call for Day to move her attention from slow ballads and jazz duets to more contemporary numbers.

The growth of rock music in the 1960s helped push Day to the sidelines musically and therefore more into the spotlight of feature films and modern music. Ironically, her son Terry Melcher was one of the most successful rock producers of the 60s, notably in the Byrds' early works and with Paul Revere and the Raiders.

By the mid-to-late 1960s, the sexual revolution instigated by the Baby Boomer generation was working to refocus the public attitude on sex. Though the times were changing, the central components of Day's feature films did not. *Do Not Disturb* in 1965 was popular with audiences, but Day's popularity was beginning to wane. Comics and critics alike dubbed Day as "The World's Oldest Virgin" as audiences increasingly shied away from her films. As a result, the last time she appeared in a Top 10 film was *The Glass Bottom Boat* in 1966.

Despite the shifting morays, Day herself refused to give up her own. When she was offered the role of Mrs. Robinson in *The Graduate*, she rejected it harshly on moral grounds. Day said she found the script to be "vulgar and offensive." The role ultimately went to Anne Bancroft, who won an Academy Award for the part.

Instead, Day moved on to shoot the western *The Ballad of Josie* in 1967. That same year, Day recorded her famous work, *The Love Album*, which was not released until 1994. It was later widely agreed that Day's *The Love Album* had been recorded at the pinnacle of her vocal prowess. It was considered by the vast majority of fans and critics alike to be her finest album. When Day heard the public's response to the album's released, she said she felt especially gratified, as she had personally hand-selected the songs.

1968

1968 was a big year for Day. She starred in the comedic take on the Northeast blackout of November 9, 1965, *Where Were You When the Lights Went Out?* Her final feature ever was also released that year, the comedy *With Six You Get Eggroll.*

April 20, 1968 is the day that Day's personal and professional lives collided in a significant way as they never had before: the death of her third husband, Marty Melcher. Though rumors had been flying for years about Marty – especially about his strained relationship with Day's son Terry, which soured after Marty had hit Terry as a child – this was the first time the public had a glimpse into Day's crumbling personal life.

Day was shocked and astonished to learn after her husband's death that not only was her fortune gone, but she was almost half a million dollars in debt. Most of this debt was owed to the IRS. Marty Melcher and Day's longtime personal lawyer Jerome Bernard Rosenthal, also Marty's business partner and advisor, had squandered Day's entire $20 million on "hair brain" get-rich-quick schemes.

Rosenthal, with a varying amount of influence and permission from Marty Melcher, had taken point on Day's financial assets and "advised" Marty to make a series of bad decisions through false, misleading, or inaccurate financial information that directly led to stupendous losses. Day filed a lawsuit against Rosenthal in February 1969 in an attempt to get her money back and won a successive decision for almost $22 million in 1974. But she didn't receive compensation until 1979, by which point most of her winnings were eaten up by debts and legal fees. As one court put it, Rosenthal had "committed breaches of professional ethics that are difficult to exaggerate."

Another significant, life-changing shock came out of Marty Melcher's death: Marty had signed Day up – against her knowledge and will and to her great displeasure – for a five-year television series. The contract itself made its own name in Hollywood history. Day's production company received millions of dollars in up-front fees on Marty's word and signature alone, while never once was Day involved in the decision making.

Said Day of the events in 1996: "It was awful, I was really, really not very well when Marty passed away, and the thought of going into TV was overpowering. But he'd signed me up for a series. And then my son Terry took me walking in Beverly Hills and explained that it wasn't nearly the end of it – I had also been signed up for a bunch of TV specials, all without anyone ever asking me."

From Big Screen to Daytime Television

Though Day despised the thought of performing on television, she felt obligated to go through with it, both for legal and promissory reasons. Day also needed the money to cover her debts to the IRS. So, on September 24, 1968, the first episode of *The Doris Day Show* aired, with "Que Sera, Sera" as its theme song. Day would spend the next five years struggling through the production process, from the grueling schedule to fights with CBS over who was allowed to maintain creative control of the show.

Although she disliked doing the show, it enjoyed a very successful five-year run, as well as serving as the curtain-raiser for *The Carol Burnett Show*. Day's program is remembered – due to her creative genius – for its abrupt, unexpected, season-to-season changes in both premise and cast. In 1969, her first full year into the show, Day received a Golden Globe for Best Actress in a Television Series due to her superb work.

By the end of *The Doris Day Show*'s final season in 1973, public tastes in culture and television changed yet again, and Day's persona became regarded as passé. Day decided to finally retire from the big screen, coming back only for occasional television specials and awards show appearances.

A Fizzling Career
and a New Life: 1970-2000

"If there is a heaven, I'm sure Rock Hudson is there because he was such a kind person." – Doris Day

Fourth Time's the Charm?

D ay's fourth and final marriage was to Barry Comden from April 14, 1976 until April 2, 1982. He was the maître d' and greeter at one of Day's favorite restaurants, the Beverly Hills Old World Restaurant. Barry appealed himself to Day by playing on her love of animals; he always had a bag of meat scraps waiting for her at the door when she was ready to leave. Shortly after their marriage, Comden came up with the idea for a line of pet food that would feature her name. Day happily embraced the idea, as she thought the profits could benefit her animal welfare work. But their stormy marriage was marred by accusations of spousal neglect, and the marriage dissolved six years later. Comden came out to say that Day had always wanted to spend more time with her dogs than with him.

After the dissolution of Day's marriage, she relocated herself and her dogs and cats to an 11-acre estate in Carmel, California, which she lovingly named Casa Loco. It was the perfect place for Day to escape from the hustle and bustle of her ever-busy life, cut off from the world by tall oak trees, covered in manicured lawns and gardens. The property even had a security fence, complete with a gatehouse and gatekeeper. After her divorce and retirement from notoriety, she rarely made public appearances, except to attend animal welfare events.

Doris Day: Her Own Story

In 1976, Day hired playwright and biographer A. E. Hotchner to write what would come to be described by himself as a "surprisingly honest" account of her life in *Doris Day – Her Own Story*. The publication of her book was the first time the public at large had a clear window to peek into her painful, dramatic private experiences, from her (at the time) three marriages to life behind the scenes. Her book's release was also the first time Doris Day officially dropped the mask that studios had built for her over the decades. The book was guaranteed a bestseller before it hit shelves, thanks to a flurry of television appearances and newspaper interviews.

The public learned for the first time Day's – and her son's – true feelings on Marty Melcher, her third husband who ruined her financially and signed her on to a television series without her knowledge or consent. Her biography laid out how Melcher, who was otherwise athletic and healthy until the few months before his death, had been diagnosed with an enlarged heart. Complications of the conditions would kill him shortly after. Most of her biography paints Melcher in an unflattering light, contrary to her previous public statements that her husband "simply trusted the wrong person" and had not intentionally engaged in wrongdoing. Her son Terry stated that the premature death of his adopted father was ultimately what saved Day from irreparable financial ruin. Actor Louis Jorden maintained to another author and biographer, David Kaufman, that Day herself had even disliked her husband at the time of his death. He also said that their marriage had crumbled to nothing more than platonic cohabitation long before Melcher was lowered into the ground.

Wrapping Up Loose Ends

Between 1985 and 1986, Day once again stepped into the land of television production with a new talk show, *Doris Day's Best Friends*, on the Christian Broadcasting Network. CBN had originally pitched a two-year contract, but despite positive worldwide publicity, the network canceled the show after only 26 episodes. Most episodes concerned Day's pastime of the previous decade: animal welfare issues.

The majority of the publicity the show did garner came from a single episode featuring Day's longtime friend and partner in television greatness, Rock Hudson. It was the first time the world got a view of the symptoms of AIDS, including severe fatigue and weight loss that was apparent even to those who didn't know.

Hudson hadn't revealed his condition to Day or the public, but it was evident from the moment he stepped into the studio that he was very sick. Despite needing rest, Hudson insisted on taping the episode. He would die from the disease a few months later, in October 1985, just days before his episode premiered.

Day took the liberty of taping a new intro into the episode before it aired. Viewers could hear her voice, choked with raw emotion, come over the tape to agree with a quote from Hudson that had struck a chord: "The best time I've ever had was making comedies with you."

Day recalled the experience as a bittersweet memory: "He was very sick, but I just brushed that off and I came out and put my arms around him and said, 'Am I glad to see you!'....We kissed goodbye, and he gave me a big hug, and he held onto me. I was in tears. That was the last time I saw him – but he's in heaven now."

October 1985 saw the beginning of the end of another haunting chapter of Day's life: the Rosenthal case. Jerome Rosenthal had been her personal lawyer from 1949, when he worked on Day's uncontested divorce from her husband, until 1968. After Marty's death, it was revealed he, with a questionable amount of help and permission from Marty, had cost Day her entire fortune and left her half a million dollars in debt.

Rosenthal and Day had been locked in the court since 1969. Day filed a lawsuit to regain more than $20 million lost to Rosenthal's shady practices and bad advice, which ended in the mid-1970s with a judgment against Rosenthal. By that point, most of that money had to go to Day's debts and legal fees, less making her whole and more breaking her even. Rosenthal wasn't satisfied with that judgment, however.

In October 1985, the California Supreme Court rejected Rosenthal's appeal of Day's successful lawsuit for legal malpractice. They upheld the conclusions of two lower courts – the original trial court and a Court of Appeals – that Rosenthal had acted "illegally and improperly." In April 1986, the United States Supreme Court refused to accept Rosenthal's next appeal to review the judgment.

Rosenthal's next step was to file his own lawsuit: $30 million against the lawyers who – he alleged – cheated him and his former client out of real estate investments worth millions of dollars. He named Day as his co-defendant, whom he described in his brief as an "unwilling, involuntary plaintiff whose consent cannot be obtained."

Rosenthal claimed that the millions of dollars Day lost were not due to his own malpractice and financial wrongdoing, but instead to real estate losses after Melcher's death. Rosenthal claimed that the attorneys who handled Day's finances after

Melcher's death had given Day bad advice: to sell three hotels in Palo Alto, California; Dallas, Texas; and Atlanta, Georgia; as well as oil leases in Kentucky and Ohio. Rosenthal claimed that the losses from these premature sales were responsible for Day's financial ruin. He claimed he had made the investments intending to keep them long-term – at least until they greatly appreciated in value. Rosenthal's brief stated that two of the three hotels had sold in 1970 for a paltry $7 million, while their estimated net worth in the year 1986 had risen to over $50 million.

Not only did Rosenthal lose this action, but the crookery of which he committed behind and during the trial would lead to his eventual disbarment.

The Legacy Years:
2000-2019

"Would you believe I am still offered scripts and projects all the time?" – Doris Day

Award...

Unlike the female stars of today, who are more and more frequently recognized for their excellence onscreen and off, much of Doris Day's recognition occurred long after she dropped out of the public eye. She received three Grammy Hall of Fame Awards in her life: one for "Sentimental Journey" in 1998, one for "Secret Love" in 1999, and one for "Que Sera, Sera" in 2012.

The same was true for much of her animal welfare work. In 2004, Day received the Presidential Medal of Freedom by sitting President George W. Bush for her accomplishments and drive in animal welfare work. Said Day at the time, "I am deeply grateful to the President and to my country.... To come from Cincinnati, Ohio, for God's sake, then to go to Hollywood, and then to get this kind of tribute from my country.... I love this country so much."

Unfortunately, Day never actually made it to the ceremony, as she had a paralyzing fear of flying. That same fear of flying is what caused Day to turn down a Kennedy Center Honors Award, as well as an honorary Academy Award. In both instances, it would have been impossible for her to make the journey on time. As a matter of fact, the last time Day appeared at any kind of awards ceremony was when she received a Golden Globe in 1989. She accepted the honor from her Carmel, California neighbor, and longtime personal friend, Clint Eastwood.

After Award...

In 2007, Day was inducted into the Hit Parade Hall of Fame to honor her most celebrated works and the sheer number of songs that made it onto various Top Ten and No. 1 lists throughout her thirty-year career.

In 2008, Tony Bennet and Natalie Cole stood in her stead to accept a Grammy for Lifetime Achievement.

In June 2010, Day received the first-ever Legend Award from the Society of Singers in Los Angeles in recognition of her lifetime's worth of achievements in the recording industry.

At age 89, on September 5, 2011, Day released *My Heart*, her first album in nearly two decades, in the UK. *My Heart* is a compilation of previously unreleased songs produced by Day's son Terry before his death. Included on the album are songs such as "You Are So Beautiful," the 1970s hit by Joe Cocker; "My Buddy," a jazzy number Day originally sang in *I'll See You in My Dreams* in 1951; and "Disney Girls" by the Beach Boys. With the album's release, Day became the oldest artist in UK history to score a UK Top 10 for an album featuring new material. After the album released in the United States, it hit No. 12 on Amazon's bestseller list. The proceeds from her latest work went to fund the Doris Day Animal League.

In January 2012, Doris received yet another honor: The Lifetime Achievement Award from the Los Angeles Film Critics Association.

And a Public Appearance

Although she had been something of a recluse for the past few decades, she made a surprise appearance at the annual namesake Doris Day Animal Foundation Benefit in April 2014.

And, although she eventually declined the role, she was in talks with Clint Eastwood about potentially joining a film he was planning to put into production in 2015.

2016 gave the public their next big surprise: a telephone interview with Day on her birthday, which had become a rarity in recent years. She also provided them with never-before-seen photos of her career and personal life, which furthered the public's continuing fascination with America's blonde sweetheart.

Day's birthday in 2017 brought another surprise – and this time, not just for the public. The Associated Press, as a birthday gift, presented Day with a copy of her birth certificate. It was then Day learned that she had been born in 1922, not 1924, as she had believed and told people all her life. Day said of her 95th birthday surprise: "I've always said that age is just a number, and I have never paid much attention to birthdays, but it's great to finally know how old I really am!"

The day after her 97th birthday in 2019 brought yet another public feeding frenzy when Day granted The Hollywood Reporter a rare interview on the Doris Day Animal Foundation. She also revealed to the world for the first time her favorite movie to make: *Calamity Jane*. Said Day of the film, "I was such a tomboy growing up, and she was such a fun character to play. Of course, the music was wonderful, too – 'Secret Love' especially is such a beautiful song."

Death: 2019

"I love to laugh. It's the only way to live. Enjoy each day – it's not coming back again!" – Doris Day

Doris Day died on May 13, 2019, after a relatively short battle with severe pneumonia. The Doris Day Animal Foundation announced her death on its website:

"Doris Day passed away early this morning at her Carmel Valley home, having celebrated her 97th birthday on April 3 of this year. Nearly 300 fans gathered in Carmel last month to celebrate Day's birthday. Day had been in excellent physical health for her age, until recently contracting a serious case of pneumonia, resulting in her death. She was surrounded by a few close friends as she passed."

Per her explicit request, the Foundation announced that there would be no funeral service, grave marker, or other public memorials. The focus would stay where she had always wanted it: on the animals.

Marriages and Personal Life: Behind the Mask

"It was the only ambition I ever had – not to be a dancer or Hollywood movie star, but to be a housewife in a good marriage."
– Doris Day

Her First Real Relationship – Or: Black and Blue

Doris Day got her first start with Barney Rapp. She auditioned with a large group of other women hoping for their chance at the spotlight, and out of more than 100 total applicants, Day got the job.

Barney Rapp himself had something of an unsavory reputation around town. He was known to have an attraction toward beautiful, underage girls – despite having a pregnant wife to return home to. While it's unclear whether Rapp and Day ever ended up in the same bed, Rapp's attitude toward young women and Day's "unusually mature" attitude about sex let speculation fly. It was not with Rapp, however, that Day dipped her toes into married life, but his trombonist, Al Jorden.

Day and Jorden met in 1940 while Day was working for Rapp. She was just 16, and he was 23. It was Jorden who first asked Day out. Day was very firmly uninterested, and she told her mother, "He's a creep, and I wouldn't go out with him if they were giving away gold nuggets at the movie!" She also described him as having one of the "glummest" personalities she had met in her short life.

Jorden was persistent, however, and eventually, Day said yes to allowing Jorden to drive her home after their shows. Alma Kappelhoff expressed her disproval of the relationship, from his surly attitude to the age difference to his potential to interfere with her career. It was not enough to hinder Day's plans of marriage and building a life. Even Jorden's bandmates warned her away from Jorden. She wouldn't heed any of them.

Day may have only been 16 years old, but she was far from naïve in the ways of men. Both of her parents were Catholic growing up; her father, a strict disciplinarian – but only with his children. Day recalled many nights when she cried herself to sleep listening to her father have affair after affair with women in his marital bed. One of these women was his wife's best friend. Though Alma divorced him when she learned the truth, it wasn't enough to keep Day from repeating her parents' mistakes and turbulent love life.

One sign her relationship with Jorden would be troubled emerged when Jorden took Day and their bandmates from Rapp's nightclub The Sign of the Drum on the Ohio River in his speedboat. Jorden attempted to max the engine racing through the giant swells given off by a passing paddleboat. The craft overturned, and everyone inside narrowly escaped a watery death when a local reporter in a passing boat came upon the accident and rescued them.

Alma begged her daughter to have nothing more to do with Jorden after the near-death experience, but Day only grew closer to Jorden. She dumped Fred Foster, a radio presenter with whom she'd been going steady for some months now (and whom she'd reportedly repeatedly toy with in the future) and agreed to marry Jorden.

Soon after, Jorden left Sign of the Drum to embark on a nationwide tour, swearing his faithfulness. Day vowed to wait for him.

After Barney Rapp turned his nightclub experience into a traveling show, Day left his band and signed on to work as a singer for the Les Brown band. She, too, traveled the country, accepting the pressures of the job with two packs of cigarettes a day and a stiff drink at the end of the night.

Although superstardom seemed to shine not far away, Day left it behind in lieu of marrying Al Jorden when he returned home, stating that she wanted to settle down. Day believed that a marriage with Jorden could provide her the stability she craved. Alma's desperate begging for her to rethink her choice did naught be cement Day's decision: she declared her career unimportant.

After dating for a year, at 17 years old, Day married Al Jorden in a New York wedding. In what might have been an indicator of the nature of the relationship, the affair was a last-minute event booked between working gigs. The reception was held at a diner located conveniently nearby.

It didn't take long for Day to discover that her marriage was not going to be all it had appeared from afar. A mere two days after the wedding, Jorden witnessed Day kiss a bandmate on the cheek in thanks for a wedding present. When he got her alone, Jorden beat her senseless.

Said Day later, "What had represented to me as love emerged as jealousy – a pathological jealousy that was destined to make a nightmare out of the next few years of my life."

That was just the first sign that Jorden was dangerously jealous of her. He believed she was having an affair or being unfaithful just for singing with other men onstage. He beat her for perceived indiscretions even as he himself repeatedly betrayed her trust and cheated on her. Day later came out to say that he called her a "dirty whore" more times than she could count. Once, they walked by a

New York City newsstand featuring a magazine with her in a swimsuit on the cover. Jorden smacked her repeatedly in the street – in front of witnesses, no less.

Day toyed with divorce frequently, only persuaded to stay by the passionate lovemaking that followed every beating.

Two months after the wedding, Day's plans to ask for a divorce were cut short when she found out she was pregnant. Jorden attempted to convince Day to get an abortion, even making an appointment with an alleyway abortionist. Day's mother herself intervened then, telling Jorden that if he forced her daughter into an abortion, Alma herself would have Jorden killed. When Day then refused to go through with the abortion, Jorden decided the child could not be his and beat her in an attempt to induce a miscarriage. It was the first of many beatings she would sustain while she was pregnant.

The idea of having a baby made Jorden more unstable and crazier than he had already been. One time, when they were alone in a car, Jorden pointed a gun at her stomach and threatened to shoot her and the baby both; Day barely managed to beg him out of it. He beat her again when they got home. Day carried a terror of riding in the front seat of a car for the rest of her life.

That was almost the end of it. While Jorden was once again traveling with his band and sleeping with his newest mistresses – after having vowed never to return – she contacted Alma. Within hours, Alma showed up with the news she had already found a house for the two of them and the baby.

Day's only child Terrence "Terry" Paul Jorden was born February 8, 1942, a mere two months later. On hearing news of Terry's birth, Jorden called Day and begged her for forgiveness – foolishly, Day agreed.

The beatings continued after Terry's birth. When Jorden was home, he refused to let Day take care of her son, to the point that he would beat her if she tried to get up to feed or comfort her baby in the night. He insisted that Alma maintain full responsibility for the child.

When he came home drunk after his latest affair, he would storm into Alma's room and rattle Terry's crib, screaming at his child, until the child screamed in return.

At 18 years old, after sustaining a second year of abuse, Day filed for divorce.

Al Jorden, who is now suspected of having been in the early throes of schizophrenia during his marriage to Day, committed suicide by firearm in 1967. Day never shed a tear.

Day once reflected that she felt no regret going through her horrendous first marriage, despite the beatings, stalking, and verbal abuse. "If I hadn't married this bird, I wouldn't have my terrific son, Terry. So, out of this awful experience came something wonderful."

The Rebound

After the dissolution of Day's marriage, she threw herself into the spotlight and started producing one musical hit after another. Her success, however, was not always dealt with gracefully. While she was considered accessible by her fans, she was also not a modest character as she gained notoriety and recognized her talents. This was often difficult for some of her peers to deal with.

Day could also throw a tantrum. It could have been due to her being only in her early twenties and already having experienced the heartbreak of an abusive, unfaithful spouse. It could have been her rising stardom and the adulation she received everywhere she went. Perhaps it was some wash of the two. She would let her temper get the best of her, resulting in slammed doors, loud swearing, and threats to leave the big studios and return home to Cincinnati.

Less than a year after leaving Jorden, Day and her raging hormones got involved with another man when she shared a hotel room with him. This was considered far more scandalous for an unmarried couple in that time. That man's name was George Weidler, a saxophonist with whom Day had worked professionally.

This time, a mortified Les Brown personally intervened. He had come to view himself as somewhat of a surrogate father figure for Day during their travels together, and he asked her to cease her relationship with Weidler. According to later statements made by Brown, he found Weidler only slightly better than Jorden as a choice. Additionally, as he reminded her at the time, fraternization amongst his band members was no longer permitted.

After Day and Weidler ignored his pleading, Brown ordered the couple to split or get. So, Weidler headed to California to make more money – after announcing he and Day were getting married.

The ceremony was held on March 30, 1946 and, as before, was slotted between gigs: George had a matinee performance in the afternoon, and Day was set to play an evening show with Brown.

Although Day once again planned to quit her career and be a stay-at-home wife and mother, she had already slotted an appearance on Bob Hope's comedic radio program, *The Popsodent Show*. Her first appearance was a great success, so they slotted another one and another after that.

Day became a regular on Bob Hope's radio program for four years. Though they initially disliked each other, they ended up as great friends and fellow comedians. Bob Hope addressed her as JB in the studio and on the air – an inside joke between them. JB stood for "Jut-Butt" on account of Day's shapely derriere.

JB was not the only nickname Day attained throughout her professional career, and almost all of them were similar inside jokes. In 1950, she earned the famous nickname "Clara Bixby" while working on *Tea for Two* with Billy De Wolfe when De Wolfe told her that she looked more like a Clara Bixby than a Doris Day. The nickname stuck, and her close friends referred to her as such until the day she died. Rock Hudson shared his own inside joke with her, nicknaming her "Eunice" because it made him laugh every time he called her that in his head.

It was Bob Hope who was responsible for introducing Day to the man who would truly make her career: Al Levy, Day's first career agent. He believed Day's talents were wasted in bands and on the radio, and that she belonged as a solo artist and on the big screen. As soon as Levy mentioned Hollywood, the land that eluded Day for so long, she perked up and asked Weidler to find them a house in Los Angeles.

When Weidler picked a trailer off an avenue filled with druggies and violence, Day was appalled and told him to try again. Matters were made worse when Day informed him that her mother would also be moving in to help care for her son Terry. Though Weidler never hit Day or Terry, he wasn't particularly fond of his stepson, and, though she wouldn't yet find out, he was cheating on Day already.

When Day realized her second marriage was failing less than a year in, she asked her new agent to get her away from her husband. Levy pulled some strings, and off to New York City Day went, with Terry and Alma in tow. Weidler, convinced his wife's rising success would continue to drive a wedge between them, wrote a letter addressed to the Little Club, where she was currently performing, demanding a divorce. When Day received the letter, she made her way back to Hollywood to talk to George in person. George finally told her he had never loved her, and it was over.

Day later reflected that "his desire not to be Mr. Doris Day" was more powerful than his desire for her.

A Complicated Life

Lonely and out of her element, Day began accompanying her agent, Al Levy, to his Hollywood gigs, as she no longer had anything holding her back. It was at one of these gigs, with many of her future costars and producers in attendance, where Day sang her famous rendition of "Embraceable You." In doing so, she inspired a couple of songwriters and a young producer to ask her to audition for a movie they had entitled *Romance on the High Seas*.

This was when Day's personal life got complicated – when she began to take actions that her music and movie studios would spend decades trying to keep under wraps.

During filming of *Romance on the High Seas*, Day started an affair with the lead male talent, Jack Carson, which was scandalous enough in its own right. Day, however, neglected to tell him that she and George Weidler were not divorced but estranged. When Weidler would visit town on performance, he and Day would spend days together in bed. To complicate things further, Day was also sleeping with her agent, Al Levy.

It was on one of these visits that Weidler apologized to Day for how he treated her and swore he'd turned a new leaf when he found religion, Christian Science. He convinced Day to join him in his spiritual pursuits. Once Day had been convinced Weidler truly wanted her back, she went to Levy. She told him that all romantic encounters would have to end and that he would have to go back to being just her agent.

For the second time in her life, Doris Day had found herself a stalker. Whenever Day went out with Weidler or Carson, Levy was there, watching from the shadows. Things came to a head when Day invited Levy to dinner, only to tell him to stop following her and accept his relegated role.

Furious, Levy followed Day back to her hotel room, where he attempted to rape her. Even for Day, who allowed more than her fair share of violence in her relationships, this was too much. She contacted Levy's business partners, Richard Dorso and Marty Melcher, at Century Artists about the encounter. Levy was given two choices: relocate to New York or have Day press charges. Beaten at last, Levy scuttled back to New York City to run that branch of Century Artists.

Next in Day's complicated romantic life came Marty Melcher, one of Levy's business partners – and her next husband. Though they weren't officially together, she began to teach him about her newest spiritual passion, Christian Science.

At this point in her life, Day was seeing multiple men at a time, unable to decide on a one: Marty Melcher, George Weidler, and Jack Carson; along with her two new additions, Steve Cochran, another handsome costar, as well as future President of the United States Ronald Reagan.

Despite all of her time and energy spent socializing, she proved herself to be a promising young star, netting thousands of dollars a week working for Warner Brothers. Her success was primarily thanks to the deals negotiated by Marty Melcher – who was reportedly obsessed with the idea of marrying her. Though he was not yet divorced from his soon-to-be ex-wife Patty Andrews (of

The Andrews Sisters), he continued to sleep with her and profess his desire. When a gossip column reported Day's affair with her manager, Patty immediately filed divorce proceedings. Melcher asked Day to marry him. She accepted and promised to give up all of the other men in her life.

Third Time's the Charm

Day and Melcher married at Burbank City Hall on April 3, 1951 – her 27th birthday. Day was ecstatic at the thought that she had finally found the one Mr. Right for her. Melcher even did what none of the other men had considered doing: he adopted her son Terry as his own. Ultimately, as with all of her romantic affairs, it was not meant to be.

Melcher became her de-facto producer and manager, and things seemed to be going well. He scored contract after contract for Day, always negotiating deals that ended with Day bringing home the big bucks. People had their suspicions about him, however. One of Day's costars, Frank Garner, thought he was a coat-riding bottom-feeder grifting off a successful woman. Frank Sinatra suspected that he wasn't all he seemed to be. Others suggested that Melcher went after Day so zealously solely for her large and growing fortune. Even Day herself had her doubts about her husband after she once caught him smacking Terry as a boy. Though they never divorced, after that day, their relationship soured.

Day's public and private comments on Melcher shifted and conflicted throughout the years. Her 1976 biography painted Melcher in an unflattering light. This was juxtaposed to her publicly stated belief that Marty had "simply trusted the wrong person" when it came to losing her fortune. Her son had no such qualms with his feelings, stating firmly that his adopted father's death was the best possible thing that could have happened to his mother, and it was Melcher's death that was ultimately responsible for saving her from total financial ruin. Actor Louis Jorden maintained to author David Kaufman that Day had long disliked her own husband.

Whatever Day's true feelings on the situation, by 1968, Day and Melcher's relationship was entirely platonic. And, after his death, all of Day's closest friends' predictions appeared to come up at least somewhat true. Marty Melcher, agent, producer, and husband of 17 years – with the help of Day's longtime personal lawyer – had blown Day's entire $20-million fortune and signed her up to a five-year television show commitment without her knowledge or consent, for a tidy upfront fee to the production company he ran numbering in the millions of dollars.

Fourth Time's the Charm?

After Melcher's death, her love life appeared to take something of a backseat to her work, first on her television show with her son, and then with her animal activist organizations. She was not entirely unsold on the prospect of love, however, and so, on April 14, 1976, she began her fourth and final marriage to the maître d' at her favorite restaurant, Barry Comden. He had worked tirelessly over months to win her affections with chilled wine on tap and a doggy bag of meat for her dogs, and at last, his efforts had come to fruition.

As with all of Day's marriages, it was tempestuous, and emotion addled. Barry frequently complained that Day preferred her pets to her people. As he told Sunday Mail in 1996: "She had 14 dogs, and the final straw was when I was kicked out of bed to make way for Tiger, a poodle."

41

Though he supported her career, even suggesting a line of dog food with her name on the front, he couldn't get behind her overwhelming desire to save all of the dogs in the world. Six years later, her fourth and final marriage was over.

Her Son's Brush with Insanity

Her son Terry was another example of how far removed her life was from the image carefully curated for her by the big-name studios.

Though she was only marginally involved, as a concerned parent, Day had high stakes in the events in the late summer of 1969. She narrowly kept her son from joining the famed, bloodbath-crazed cult of Charles Manson, while at the same time mitigating a financial fiasco. The information that comes to the public was routed through the Manson trial transcripts, as well as firsthand accounts from Beach Boys member Mike Love. Love detailed in writing the strange nature of the three-way friendship that formed from 1967 to 1969 between Charles Manson, Love's bandmate Dennis Wilson, and Terry Melcher.

Melcher was a record producer at the time, a big name in the game of rock n roll, and a close friend of Dennis Wilson. When Wilson got chummy with Charles Manson – who was trying to break his way into the Hollywood music scene at the time – he introduced Manson to Melcher. Manson had high hopes of convincing Melcher to sign him to a record deal and give him the big break he sought.

As Manson wasn't up to par with the level of clientele Melcher currently produced for, Melcher put off signing repeatedly. He remained friendly with the so-called "Manson family," however. He even visited Manson at his famed ranch in the summer of 1969, the same ranch where blood would fly and victims would fall prey to the violent charms of the Manson family.

At that time, Melcher was dating a woman named Candance Bergen, a real up-and-coming Hollywood star. They lived together in a modest rental house located in Benedict Canyon at 10050 Cielo Drive.

Wilson and Manson both regularly visited Bergen and Melcher at that house frequently. According to bandmate Mike Love, it was Doris Day who first raised the alarm at the deepening friendship between the volatile Manson and her swept-up son Terry. After much begging and pleading with her son, she convinced Terry that he needed to move his girlfriend out of that house. So, in January 1969, they left.

Charles Manson was aware that the couple had moved, but throughout his many visits to the house and continuing denials of a record deal from Melcher, he had fixed that house in his head as a locus of Hollywood power and import and betrayal – as the center of Hollywood's ultimate iniquity.

June 1969 proved to be the last straw. Melcher told Manson for the final time that he couldn't sign Manson to a record deal – and Manson was not happy.

On August 8, 1969, Manson directed his bloodthirsty followers to attack Hollywood itself: the residence at 10050 Cielo Drive. Instead of finding Melcher and Bergen as planned, Manson's followers found Roman Polanski's pregnant wife Sharon Tate hosting a party with some of her friends.

Melcher, who was deeply disturbed and riddled with guilt over the experience, was only able to testify at the trial while under sedation.

Though Day was only indirectly involved, the story of her son's near involvement with a cult stood as a vivid testament to the changing times. It also served as a testament to undermine the myth of her persona.

Sexuality and Public Image

"I'm tired of being thought of as Miss Goody Two-shoes.... I'm not the All-American Virgin Queen, and I'd like to deal with the true, honest story of who I really am." -Doris Day

Day fascinated and allured audiences around the world with her presentation of the enticing, chaste-until-marriage sexual virgin. This was an oxymoron that she proudly clung to onscreen, even as her personal life would fall apart time and again. Day and her characters had "a way" about her, drawing men in with a great sense of sensuality and showing them the door before they made it to the bedroom. Perhaps one of the more subtle and emblematic examples is in *Two for Two*, in which Day crooned a sultry, suggestive-but-not-sexual version of a song about two lovers on a romantic getaway – to her uncle.

Though she wasn't the pure 1950's housewife dream, even in her movies – most of her characters had a career, often to the chagrin of their husbands – she was every man's "proper" desire from an era that never really existed. All of her comedic roles had a distinct formula meant to reward the virgins of America for holding out: a cheeky, assertive, conservative woman who would captivate the hearts and minds of men, luring them into abandoning their playboy lifestyles in favor of a marriage proposal. Critic Pauline Kael dubbed it "the Doris Day routine of flirting with bed but never getting there."

Although she was the archetype of mid-19th century femininity and modernity, she maintained a static persona. Her head looked to the future even as her feet remained firmly planted in a nonexistent past. Her onscreen model was the epitome of ideal womanhood. Throughout her career, her image and popularity would wax and wane as cultural norms grew more open and sexual taboos became commonplace.

Even in her sauciest films, Day clung to the sexual appeal that men found came with "proper" womanly chastity. 1959's *Pillow Talk* found Day flirting with two men, while at the same time expressing over-the-top horror and disgust when she was met with a bachelor pad and insinuations of sex before marriage.

She and fellow actor – and leading man in some of her more famous roles – Rock Hudson portrayed an image of heteronormative Americana that never existed for either of them. Rock Hudson was a closeted queer man who would later die of AIDS, while Day continually struggled with violent, abusive men in her relationships while attempting to contain a hold on her financial and professional destinies. Their offscreen lives complicated their legacies, as well as the legacy and truth behind the picture of "classic America" that conservative members of society clung to long into the sexual and cultural revolution of the 1960s.

Day later revealed that she sometimes felt she existed in a parallel world of "sexless" sex comedies, embodying a manufactured innocence of the 1950s that even she never believed in. As she told her biographer A. E. Hotchner in *Doris Day: Her Own Story*: "My public image is unshakably that of America's wholesome virgin, the girl next door, carefree and brimming with happiness. An image, I can assure you, more make-believe that any film part I ever played."

Even if she never believed in the product she peddled, she wore her brand proudly. This was exemplified when Mike Nichols attempted to cast her as his leading lady in *The Graduate*, only to be turned down harshly. This now-famous film, about an older woman who repeatedly and forcibly seduces her daughter's 20-something-year-old boyfriend, "offended my [Day's] sense of values."

As time wore on and the cultural revolution of the 1960s turned into the war-addled era that was the 1970s, Day became somewhat of a cultural joke about the pure, sexual woman. Comedic pianist Oscar Levant famously joked that he "knew Doris Day before she was a virgin," in what could be the most straightforward summation of the 1960s attitude about women, sex, and Doris Day herself.

Though her wholesome girl-next-door image was criticized during the feminist movements in the 1960s, not everyone saw her as remnants of a time gone by. Film critic Molly Haskell wrote in a 1976 essay to Ms. Magazine that Day was a "proto-feminist" who "challenged, in her working-woman roles, the limited destiny of women to marry, live happily ever after, and never be heard from again."

Animal Activism

"I'm going to do as much as I can for the animal world, and I'll never stop." – Doris Day

An Old Passion

Doris Day was one of the most dedicated figures to ever advocate for animal rights and welfare. Notably, she began long before it was considered a public norm to show compassion or have a cause in favor of the animals. Day protected and defended animals and those who loved them until the day she died. She was a passionate animal lover, and it was said she believed she had an innate connection with them. Animals seemed to relate to her immediately, and she said that she recognized the gentility in their souls. She considered them to be spiritual creatures with a unique capacity for unconditional love.

Day's interest in animal welfare began in her teenage years when her dog Tiny ran out into the street while on a walk and was struck dead by a car. Day was in the middle of her recovery from her double compound leg fracture and unable to chase after him and save him. She often afterward expressed guilt and loneliness about Tiny's death.

Throughout her acting career, she was very compassionate toward animals, but it wasn't a central focus for her until later into her fame. Though she had the clout to throw around, it wasn't until 1956 that she finally pulled rank to protect animals publicly. But she did so in Morocco.

Day was working on the set of Alfred Hitchcock's *The Man Who Knew Too Much*, cast as the leading lady opposite Jimmy Stewart – a fellow animal lover and advocate. She surprised everyone when she suddenly put her foot down and declared that she refused to continue filming and production unless the starving, emaciated animals near the set received proper care and food. Within days, the production company had set up a feeding station for a wide assortment of animals, including burros, cows, cats, dogs, goats, horses, and lambs, among others. Day supervised the feed and other care provided. Satisfied with the results of her intervention, the filming finished uninterrupted.

When Doris Day left Hollywood at the conclusion of *The Doris Day Show*, it was for good – minus the occasional special occasion appearance. She never looked back (to showbiz, anyway). Day branched out into a new, more fulfilling career with the same incredible energy and vivacious enthusiasm that had once catapulted her to the top of her entertainment profession: promoting positive animal welfare. She worked tirelessly to rescue, care for, and place thousands of abused and neglected animals, both by her own hand and through her network.

A New Career

Day helped co-found the grassroots organization "Actors and Others for Animals" in the 1970s, often going door to door to rescue pets in distress and collect donations. She appeared in newspaper advertisements denouncing fur clothing alongside Mary Tyler Moore, Jayne Meadows, and Angie Dickinson.

In 1978, Day went on to found the Doris Day Pet Foundation so she could focus on an issue of more immediate importance to her: finding homes for the animals who were destroyed because there weren't enough homes. DDPF was established as a non-profit,

501(c)(3) organization, authorizing it to accept and give grants as a public service charity. DDPF continues to operate independently even after her death, promoting its cause and funding – or finding funding for – other organizations that share their mission of bringing animals and the people who love them together.

Day fostered many animals at her own home to aid with the efforts, leased space for more kennels, and cultivated a large, and growing, staff of volunteers to help her find homes for the large number of homeless animals she encountered. Some of these animals happened to be in her path. Some of them were more intentionally placed.

It was not uncommon for people passing through the neighborhood to drop animals over Day's property walls, or even over her front gate. Others who were familiar with her daily routine would wait outside her gates until she got home and hand over the animals themselves. Sometimes, she would open her front gate to leave for the day and find another cat or dog with a note attached. Although she told everyone around her that she felt accomplished and fulfilled, the sheer number of animals grew too overwhelming for both herself and her foundation to handle.

That didn't stop her from trying. One star was famously quoted as saying, "We all had at least one of 'those Doris Day animals.' If you saw Doris on the street or at the studio, chances are you would end up with some homeless cat or dog Doris was sponsoring. She carried around photos of the animals who needed homes, and then she'd actually come over to inspect your house to make sure you were up to it."

Even as the famous and rich filled their houses with "those Doris Day animals," there were more pouring into her shelters and over her walls by the day. As Day came to consider the root cause of the animal crisis, she turned her focus to the core: pet overpopulation through overbreeding. Thus, nine years after she founded the Doris Day Pet Foundation, she became president and founding member of her newest and proudest accomplishment: the Doris Day Animal League, a lobbying organization for laws regulating the ethical breeding and treatment of animals.

Political Activism

Doris Day was very active in her namesake organization, and as a result, the Animal League was overwhelmingly successful. Whatever was needed, wherever her presence was required, whoever she had to write or call, Day was present. On the phone, dictating letters, speaking in person and on the record to anyone who would listen - if it had to be done, Day did it.

Far from being a shy presence, she made herself known up to the highest levels of government: The President of the United States. Ronald Reagan knew her by name, first from starring with her in two films during his acting days, and then again as a brutal force of nature vying for a cause held dear. Reagan learned of her zeal and determination firsthand when she called him personally to "discuss" the fact that he had exiled one of his dogs to the Western White House.

Day herself went to Washington, D.C., among local jurisdictions, to lobby the Congress of the United States on behalf of legislation regarding the safeguarding of animal welfare on multiple occasions. She pursued causes from required spay and neutering ordinances in large cities and counties to mandates on humane treatment for farm and slaughterhouse animals to limiting and regulating animal testing for cosmetics and other human health and beauty products.

Members of Congress, in turn, came to Day when they needed support for related legislation. She was approached to give her view on legislator's opinions and issues plaguing their home states, as well as the status and involvement of relevant national pet welfare legislation. City councils would contact her to get her endorsement on animal welfare bills they hoped to push through. Cities, states, and countries lobbied for her approval. Day received invitations to attend events and fundraisers held all over the world.

In 2006, the Animal League incorporated as the lobbying base on behalf of animal rights for the Humane Society of the United States. The Humane Society now manages World Spay Day, a continuance of the Spay Day USA that Day had pioneered in the year 1995. The Doris Day Animal Foundation remained an independent entity and welfare charity, working with the Humane Society as needed but maintaining separate funding and influence. Doris Day herself assisted in operations until shortly before her death.

Activism into Old Age

In 2009, Day funded the Doris Day Animal Horse Rescue Facility at the Cleveland Amory Black Beauty Horse Ranch in Murchison, Texas. The ranch was named for her late friend, Cleveland Amory, who began the project before his death. Cleveland Amory served as Day's inspiration to continue the project. Day fulfilled his dream and legacy with a personal $250,000 donation to fund the center's founding. Over 250 neglected and abused horses were rescued from western Nebraska and placed at the ranch for healing and rehabilitation.

Day herself rescued a horse, Mocha, through the SPCA of Monterey, California. Day made sure her Foundation contributed to Mocha's upkeep as she climbed up in her years. When she visited him at the SPCA center, the staff received a pleasant shock. Every horse in the center was immediately drawn to Day, coming over to give their greetings and receive her loving attention in return. The SPCA staff commented that they had never seen their horses so affectionate with any creature, human or otherwise.

Doris Day: Favorites

In order to truly know Doris Day, it's important to take a look at some of her work – not only her best performances, but the ones that had a part to play in turning a young girl with a battered past into a worldwide symbol of sensuality and womanhood.

Calamity Jane

Day's personal favorite movie, as she revealed in an interview with The Hollywood Reporter the day after her 97th birthday, was *Calamity Jane*. As she said at the time: "...she was such a fun character to play. Of course, the music was wonderful, too."

Calamity Jane was not only fun for her to film, but the movie netted Day her first ever Oscar. She won Best Song for her performance of "Secret Love" during the 1953 Academy Awards (and a Grammy Hall of Fame Award for the song in 1999). Day wrote in her biography, *Doris Day, Her Own Story*, that the first time she heard "Secret Love" it was so beautiful she "almost fainted."

The recording of "Secret Love" was something special too, as it was only done once. In her biography, Day laid out how, on the afternoon of the recording day, she rode her bike to the studio, sang the song for the first time with the studio orchestra, and then was called into the recording booth with the musical director. As Day wrote in her biography: "[He] said, 'That's it. You're never going to do it better.'"

The Man Who Knew Too Much and "Que Sera, Sera"

The Man Who Knew Too Much was important in Doris Day's life for several reasons. It was during production that she famously asked Alfred Hitchcock why she was receiving no direction, only for his response to be that she didn't require it. It was also the first time that Day showed a public affection for animals, with her famous episode of halting filming until the starving animals outside the set were given food and basic medical care. *The Man Who Knew Too Much* was Day's tenth Top 10 box office hit, and its famous song saw the Academy Award for Best Original Song go to songwriters Jay Livingston and Ray Evans.

In addition to being perhaps the most famous performance of her career, out of its production came one of her most famous songs, the very one the Livingston and Evans won an Oscar for: "Que Sera, Sera (Whatever Will Be, Will Be)."

To everyone's great surprise, Day didn't like the song at first, and it never became a favorite for her. Initially, her concerns lied with where the song was going to fit into the movie, as she didn't see it fitting with the plot. After the movie's release, however, the song proved so popular with crowds that Day began to see it in a different light. Said Day in an interview to NPR, "...it was for our child in the movie. Then I realized, maybe it isn't a favorite song of mine, but people loved it, and kids loved it, and it was perfect for the film....boy, it sure did something."

"Que Sera, Sera" brought Day adoration and adulation throughout her career, but it wasn't until 2012 that she was officially recognized for its success. That year saw Day receive her third Grammy Hall of Fame Award for her most famous song.

"Day by Day"

Though it rarely made a splashy appearance in her famous years, "Day by Day" is inarguably one of the most influential songs of Day's life. It was on her first ever radio show that Day belted out the lyrics that would only a few short months later earn Day her famous surname. Technically, her now-iconic performance on *Carlin's Carnival* was the first time Day ever performed publicly at all. Despite its important place in Day's life, however, the song never brought her any acclaim and glory beyond her earliest years in the spotlight.

It was 30 years later when Day admitted that she didn't care for her famous moniker. "I think it's a phony name," she said. "I never did like it. Still don't."

"Sentimental Journey"

"Sentimental Journey" was the first hit of Day's singing career, and it is the song ultimately responsible for Day being recognized as a vocal artist. The song came out of her 1944 stint working with Les Brown and his band. The fame of "Sentimental Journey" is partially due to its coincidental timing with World War II. Soldiers abroad and grieving mothers at home alike adopted the song as an anthem to end the bloodshed and bring the troops home. Unlike "Day by Day," Day would return to record "Sentimental Journey" several times throughout her career. "Sentimental Journey" netted Day one of her three Grammy Lifetime Awards in the year 1998.

In addition to being a big hit for Day, the song would later become a big hit for some big-name stars, including Buck Clayton, Ben Sidran, and Frank Sinatra. One of Day's favorite stars and biggest inspirations, Ella Fitzgerald, even recorded a cover in 1947.

Printed in Great Britain
by Amazon